OUR BODIES

THE HEART, LUNGS AND BLOOD

Steve Parker

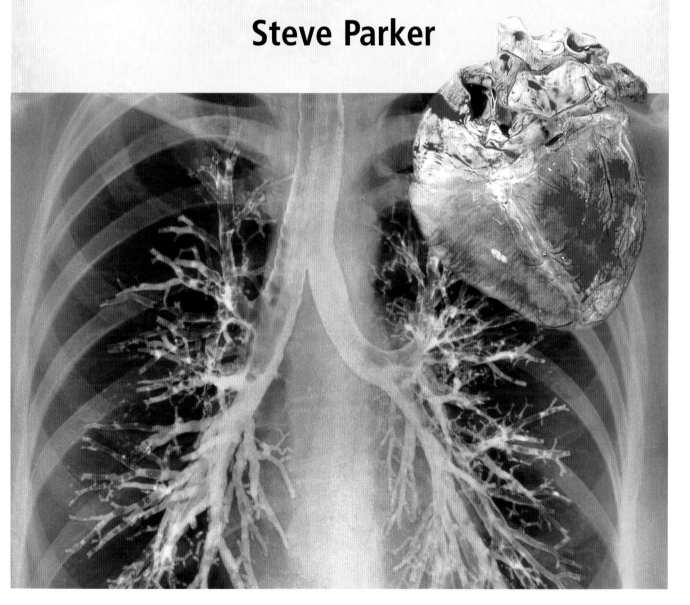

HODDER
Wayland

an imprint of Hodder Children's Books

Titles in the series:
The Brain and Nervous System • Digestion
The Heart, Lungs and Blood • Reproduction
The Senses • The Skeleton and Muscles

Produced by Monkey Puzzle Media Ltd
Gissing's Farm, Fressingfield, Suffolk IP21 5SH, UK

Text copyright © 2003 Steve Parker
Series copyright © 2003 Hodder Wayland
First published in 2003 by Hodder Wayland
an imprint of Hodder Children's Books

Commissioning Editor: Victoria Brooker
Book Editor: Nicola Edwards
Design: Jane Hawkins
Picture Research: Lynda Lines
Artwork: Alex Pang
Consultant: Dr Trish Groves

British Library Cataloguing in Publication Data
Parker, Steve
  The heart, lungs and blood. - (Our bodies)
  1.Heart - Juvenile literature 2.Lungs - Juvenile literature
  3.Blood - Circulation - Juvenile literature
  I.Title
  612.1

ISBN 07502 3673 6

Printed and bound in Italy

Hodder Children's Books
A division of Hodder Headline Ltd
338 Euston Road, London NW1 3BH

Picture Acknowledgements
Corbis Digital Stock 31 top; FLPA 7 (R Van Nostrand), 15 (Albert Visage), 29 bottom (Minden Pictures), 33 top (E & D Hosking), 41 right (Minden Pictures); MPM Images 10; Robert Harding Picture Library front cover main image, 4 (Nakamura), 11, 12, 23 (Yoav Levy, Phototake), 37 bottom (Louise Murray), 41 left (Phototake), 45; Science Photo Library front cover inset (Innerspace Imaging), 1 (Innerspace Imaging), 1 inset (John Radcliffe Hospital), 5 (Deep Light Productions), 8 (Innerspace Imaging), 9 (Hossler, Custom Medical Stock Photo), 14 (Prof. C Ferlaud), 16 (Manfred Kage), 17 (Crown Copyright/Health & Safety Laboratory), 19 left (Quest), 19 right (BSIP, Laurent), 20 (Simon Lewis), 25 (Biology Media), 26 (Alex Bartel), 27 (BSIP, Vem), 29 top (John Radcliffe Hospital), 31 bottom (CC Studio), 33 bottom (D Phillips), 34 (BSIP, Chassenet), 37 top (James King-Holmes), 38 (PHT), 42 (Adam Hart-Davis), 43 (Mehau Kulyk), 44 (Geoff Tompkinson); Topham Picturepoint 35 (ImageWorks).

CONTENTS

INTRODUCTION

Two vital processes

A human body can only stay alive if two processes happen every second, of every minute, hour after hour, year after year. The body has to breathe and its heart has to beat. These processes are so important for life that they are known as vital signs. In a serious accident or injury, experts such as paramedics check these vital signs first.

BREATHING

Breathing is done by the nose, windpipe, and the airways and lungs in the chest. Together they form the respiratory system. Its job is to take fresh air into the body, and obtain from it the gas called oxygen, which passes into the blood. Oxygen makes up about one-fifth of air. It is an essential part of the body's chemistry because it helps to break apart high-energy substances from food, especially glucose sugar ('blood sugar'). The released energy drives all body processes, including muscle-powered movements, digestion, getting rid of wastes, the heart's beating, thinking in the brain and even breathing itself.

Oxygen gas is so essential for the human body that, where it is lacking, we must take our own supplies.

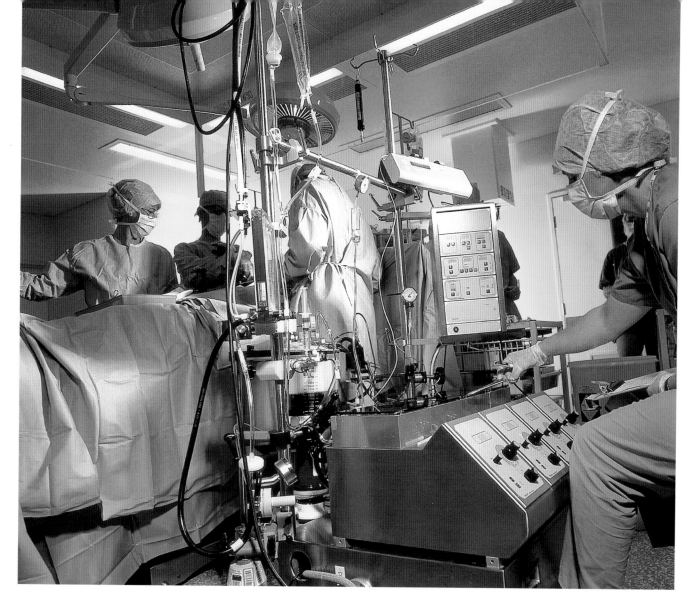

HEART AND CIRCULATION

Oxygen is taken into the lungs by the respiratory system. But it is spread around the body by the circulatory system – the heart, blood vessels (tubes) and blood. The heart is positioned between the two lungs, in the chest. It is a muscular pump that forces blood to flow through the network of blood vessels so that it reaches every part of the body. Unlike food, blood does not enter the body at one end and leave at the other. The same blood flows round and round, or circulates, through the blood vessels.

In hospital, life-support 'heart-lung' machines can take over the jobs of breathing and circulation for a short time. This allows surgeons to operate on the heart.

ESSENTIAL WORK

In addition to carrying vital oxygen, blood delivers energy-containing sugars, important nutrients and many other substances to all body parts. It also collects wastes for removal. Together the respiratory and circulatory systems keep the body supplied with oxygen, energy and much more. If these systems stop for just a few minutes, life ceases.

THE RESPIRATORY SYSTEM

Main parts

The respiratory system has these main parts: the nose and throat, the windpipe or trachea, the main airways or bronchi, plus the two lungs. The nose is the main way in for fresh, oxygen-rich air heading down towards the lungs, and the main way out for stale or 'used' air coming back up from the lungs.

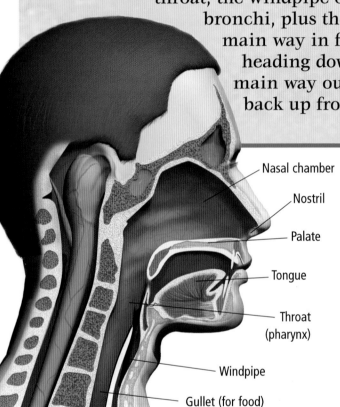

Nasal chamber

Nostril

Palate

Tongue

Throat (pharynx)

Windpipe

Gullet (for food)

The nasal chambers are two large cavities behind the nose. Their floor or palate is also the roof of the mouth.

THE NOSE

The nose is specially designed to change incoming air, to make it more suitable for the lower parts of the respiratory system. Air flows through the nostrils into the two nasal chambers, where the moist lining makes the air damp, so that it doesn't dry out the lower airways and lungs. There are also many blood vessels in the lining of the nose which warm incoming air if it is cold. The hairs in the nose, and the sticky mucus (slime) produced by the lining, filter and clean the air by trapping bits of floating dust and germs.

Top Tips

The nose is designed to warm and humidify (dampen) incoming air, and remove dust and germs. But sometimes, air is very dirty or dusty. Wearing a face mask can help to filter out unwanted particles. People wear breathing masks when cycling in a crowded city, or when using tools such as grinders and sanders.

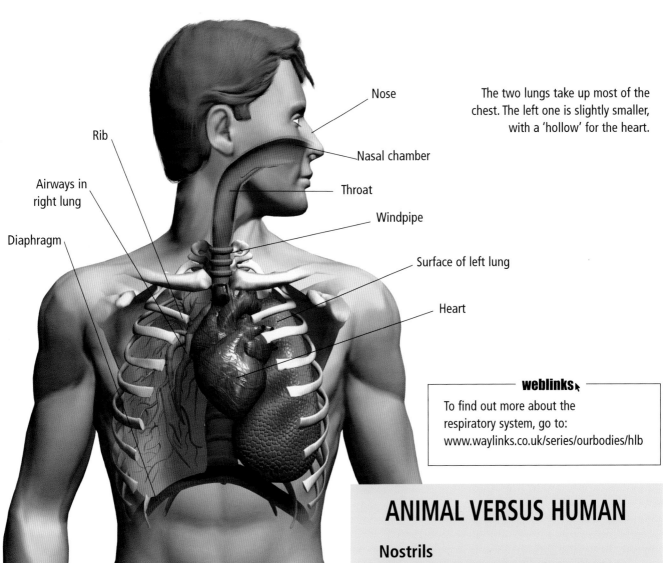

Nose

Nasal chamber

Throat

Windpipe

Surface of left lung

Heart

Rib

Airways in right lung

Diaphragm

The two lungs take up most of the chest. The left one is slightly smaller, with a 'hollow' for the heart.

weblinks
To find out more about the respiratory system, go to:
www.waylinks.co.uk/series/ourbodies/hlb

THE THROAT AND WINDPIPE

The rear of the nose leads to the throat and voice box, and down into the windpipe. This is a wide, flexible tube which carries air through the neck and upper chest to the lungs. It has stiff C-shaped hoops of springy cartilage (gristle) in its walls, to hold it open. Without this support, natural pressure inside the body and the twists and bends of the neck would squash and close the windpipe.

ANIMAL VERSUS HUMAN

Nostrils
Whales and dolphins have their nostrils on top of their heads! The nostrils form an opening called the blowhole. This allows them to breathe in air by poking just the top of their heads out of the water.

This dolphin is breathing not through its mouth, but through its blowhole, which will close as it dives.

The windpipe branches

After fresh air passes in through the nose, and down the throat and windpipe, it reaches a two-way fork. Here the windpipe branches into two main air tubes, called bronchi. One bronchus leads to the right lung, and the other to the left lung. After another 5–10 centimetres each bronchus divides again, and then again, becoming thinner each time – like a tree trunk dividing into branches and twigs. After about 15 divisions, the original wide bronchus has branched into tens of thousands of tiny bronchioles. These are thinner than human hairs and reach into all parts of the lungs.

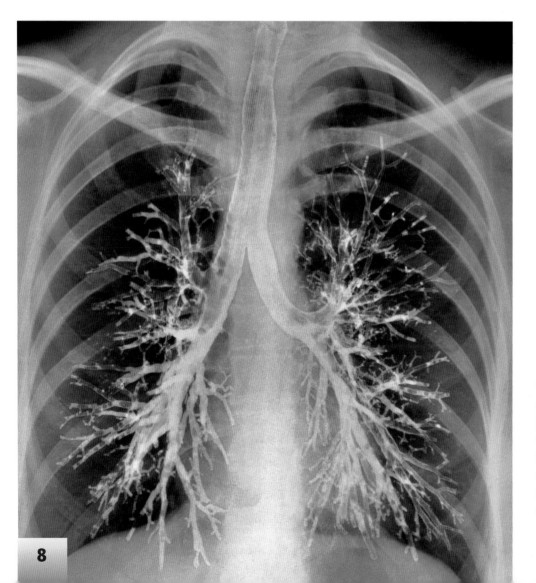

This X-ray image shows the two main airways or bronchi, branching from the windpipe. Each bronchus divides many times within the lungs, becoming narrower with each division.

AIR BUBBLES

At the end of each bronchiole is a group of microscopic air bubbles called alveoli. They have very thin walls, and covering them is a network of microscopic blood vessels, called capillaries. The distance from the air inside each alveolus to the blood around it, is 20 times less than the thickness of a sheet of paper. Oxygen can seep easily from the air into the blood, to be carried away around the body. At the same time a waste gas in the blood, carbon dioxide, passes the other way, into the air in the alveolus. It is removed from the body when the air is breathed out.

Bunches of alveoli are attached to terminal bronchioles, like grapes hanging from a stalk. The capillaries around them are so numerous, that at any moment the lungs contain up to one-fifth of all the blood in the body.

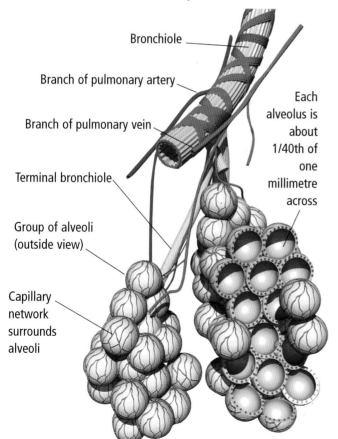

Bronchiole

Branch of pulmonary artery

Branch of pulmonary vein

Terminal bronchiole

Group of alveoli (outside view)

Capillary network surrounds alveoli

Each alveolus is about 1/40th of one millimetre across

MICRO-BODY

There are more than 300 million alveoli in each lung. They give the lung a soft, spongy feel, and provide it with a huge surface area for taking in oxygen. Spread out flat, the alveoli in both lungs would cover the area of 30 single beds, or a whole tennis court.

Alveoli are like micoscopic balloons squashed together. Air passes in and out of them through tiny tubes, the bronchioles.

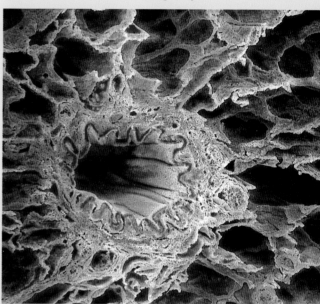

Try this!

Breathe out onto a cold mirror, or into the cold air on a winter's day. You'll see a fine mist which is formed by water droplets coming out of the lungs as water vapour. The moisture comes from the damp lining of the alveoli and airways. Every day the lungs lose about half a litre of body water in this way.

BREATHING

Muscles

Breathing uses two main sets of muscles. One is a large, sheet-like muscle called the diaphragm, directly underneath the lungs. The others are the intercostals, which are long, strap-like muscles, one between each pair of rib bones.

To drink through a straw, muscles force the lungs to become larger. This lowers the pressure of air inside them. The outside air pressure is then higher than the lungs' air pressure and pushes the drink up the straw.

BREATHING IN

Inspiration or breathing in uses muscle power. The diaphragm muscle is dome-shaped, curving up below the lungs. When it gets shorter or contracts, it becomes flatter. This pulls the bases of the lungs down and makes the lungs bigger, stretching them like a sponge. At the same time, the intercostals pull on the ribs and make them tilt, swinging up and forwards. This also stretches the lungs. As the lungs enlarge, they suck in fresh air from outside.

Top Tips

Hiccups happen when the diaphragm works suddenly on its own, causing a sudden in-breath. They may happen when we eat or drink too much and the full stomach presses on the diaphragm just above.

There are many ideas on how to stop hiccups, such as holding your breath, or sipping water slowly from a cup.

BREATHING OUT

Expiration or breathing out uses almost no muscle power. Both the diaphragm and intercostals relax. This takes the pulling force off the stretched lungs. Being naturally elastic, the lungs spring back to their normal smaller size, puffing out 'used' air.

BREATHING POWER

Blowing uses muscles under the chest and around the front of the abdomen (belly), as well as normal breathing muscles. They tighten and press on the stomach and guts, which in turn press on the diaphragm and lungs above. Sucking uses shoulder muscles, which raise the top of the chest and stretch the lungs more than normal.

ANIMAL VERSUS HUMAN

A frog breathes with its chin! A frog's chin has a large, thin sheet of skin which is worked by muscles. It curves in and out, pushing air down into the lungs and then sucking it out.

A frog can push air up from its lungs to make its chin sac balloon out.

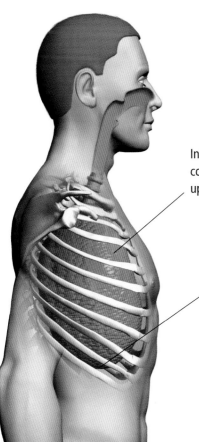

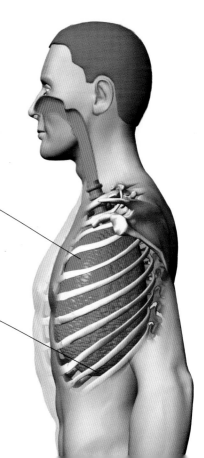

The muscles of breathing pull or contract to make the lungs larger (left), to breathe in. Breathing out uses little muscle power as the stretched lungs spring back to their smaller size (right).

Intercostal muscles contract to raise ribs up and outwards

Intercostal muscles relax and allow ribs to tilt down and inwards

Diaphragm contracts and flattens

Diaphragm relaxes and curves up

weblinks

To find out more about breathing, go to: www.waylinks.co.uk/series/ourbodies/hlb

RUNNING A RACE

WARMING-UP

A race is about to start! The body prepares for a burst of action, when its muscles will work hard to run to the finish line. First, it's important to warm up all the muscles with exercises such as stretching and jogging.

These exercises apply to the breathing muscles as well, so a warm-up includes taking deep breaths. When the muscles get busy, they will need extra energy and oxygen. So the respiratory system must work harder, to take in more oxygen, more quickly.

The pleural membrane is a single bag-like sheet, folded in on itself to make two almost touching layers, that wrap all around each lung.

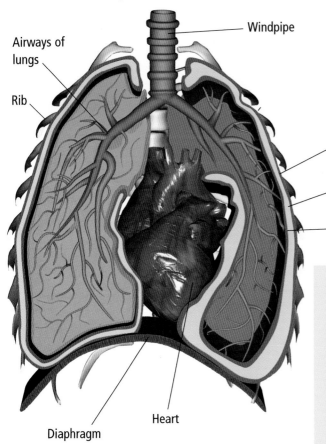

Windpipe

Airways of lungs

Rib

Outer pleural layer

Pleural fluid between layers

Inner pleural layer

Diaphragm

Heart

HOW MUCH AIR?

During normal breathing, each breath moves about half a litre of air in and out of the lungs. When the body is active, the amount is much greater. In a large adult it can reach more than four litres of air with each deep breath.

HOW FAST DO YOU BREATHE?

The rate or speed of breathing also increases during exercise. At rest, there are 12–15 breaths (in-and-out) each minute. During exercise this can rise to 60 or more breaths per minute. This means more than 200 litres of air move in and out of the lungs each minute, compared to less than 10 litres at rest. Breathing speed and depth are controlled by the brain (see page 36).

MICRO-BODY

The lungs are covered by a thin, oily, slippery 'bag' called the pleural membrane. This lets the lungs slide inside the chest, as they become bigger and smaller with each breath. In the illness called pleurisy, the layer becomes swollen and sore, and every breath is painful.

The voice box

Every breath sends air through the voice box, or larynx. This is in the front of the neck, between the throat above and the windpipe below. Inside are two stiff strips that stick out, one on each side, like thin shelves. They are called vocal cords or vocal folds, and they make the sounds of your voice.

QUIET BREATHING

The voice box is made from curved plates of tough, bendy cartilage. The biggest of these forms a bulge, the 'Adam's apple', at the front of the neck. (Both males and females have the Adam's apple, but it is usually more noticeable in adult males.) The cartilage plates support the vocal cords and are moved by neck muscles.

Try this!

The vocal cords are angled up slightly so that they work best when breathing out, as air leaves the lungs. Try to speak while you're breathing in. It's much more difficult!

This view into the throat with a laryngoscope (a telescope-like device) shows the vocal cords or folds pulled together for speech, with a narrow slit between them for air to pass.

During normal breathing, the vocal cords are apart. They form a V-shaped hole, wider at the back than the front, called the glottis. Air flows through this without a sound as you breathe.

NOISY TALKING

When a person speaks, muscles move the vocal cords together so that they almost touch. Air flows up through the narrow slit between them, and makes them shake fast or vibrate. The vibrations create the sound of the voice. To make the sound higher in pitch, the muscles stretch the vocal cords longer and tighter. For a louder sound, the lungs send up more air faster. As the sounds come up and out, they are altered by air spaces in the nose and mouth, and by the positions of the tongue, cheek and lips. This is how you form clearly-spoken words and why you have a unique voice.

Base of tongue

Epiglottis

False vocal cord

Cartilage of larynx

Vocal cord

Glottis (gap between cords)

Windpipe

This view from the rear (through the back of the neck) shows the voice box cut away to reveal the vocal cords, which are infoldings on each side of the airway.

ANIMAL VERSUS HUMAN

The champion noise-maker on land is the howler monkey of South America. Its great whoop is made even louder by its huge voice box and throat. Its treetop howls can be heard more than five kilometres away.

Howler monkeys whoop and yell at dawn and dusk, to warn other howlers to stay away.

BREATHING PROBLEMS

Body reactions

Breathing is so important that the body has many automatic, natural reactions to keep it going. If an object gets into the throat or windpipe, the chest and abdomen muscles suddenly blast air at high pressure, up from the lungs and out through the mouth. This action, known as a cough, usually makes the vocal cords rattle as it blows the object out of the airway system.

AH-TISH-OO!

A sneeze is similar to a cough, except that the air blasts out through the nose. Sneezing can be caused by dusty air, or by too much mucus inside the nose, due to a cold or an allergy such as hay fever. An allergy is when the body reacts to a substance which is normally harmless – in the case of hay fever, tiny floating particles such as plant pollen.

BREATHING DIFFICULTIES

Sometimes the air tubes in the lungs narrow, making breathing difficult and wheezy. This can also be caused by an allergy. The wheezing and shortness of breath is known as asthma. A medicine breathed in, from an inhaler, widens the air tubes again and relieves the asthma. Another kind of medicine can be breathed in regularly to prevent asthma.

MICRO-BODY

In the lung condition emphysema, the tiny alveoli (air bubbles) become weak, stretching and merging into bigger, thicker-walled air spaces. This causes shortness of breath, because there is less area to take in oxygen and a thicker barrier for it to get through.

Emphysema, where the alveoli lose shape and merge together, is one of many diseases linked to smoking.

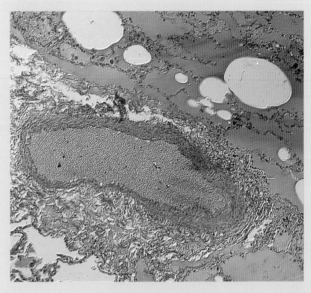

GERMS IN THE SYSTEM

The delicate linings of the respiratory system can be invaded by germs (harmful microbes such as bacteria and viruses). This may lead to infections, including colds in the nose, bronchitis in the main airways, and pneumonia in the smallest air tubes and alveoli. Influenza or 'flu often starts like a bad cold but can affect the main airways and lungs, too. The body can usually fight off a cold or even influenza, but medicines may be needed for serious cases and for bronchitis or pneumonia.

No smoking!

Smoke from cigarettes and pipes causes serious and long-term harm to many parts of the respiratory system. It can cause infections, growths and cancers, and similar problems in other parts of the body.

weblinks

To find out more about breathing problems, go to: www.waylinks.co.uk/series/ourbodies/hlb

Face masks help to protect against dust and floating particles, which not only clog the delicate airways and alveoli in the lungs, but may also cause scarring and cancerous changes.

THE CIRCULATORY SYSTEM

Two routes

After oxygen enters the blood it travels through the circulatory system. The blood is sent around the body, to deliver essential oxygen to every tiny part. But there are actually two routes for the blood to circulate – the pulmonary circulation and systemic circulation.

COLLECTING OXYGEN

The pulmonary journey is from the heart to the lungs and back. It's very quick, since the heart is directly between the lungs, and the blood vessels (tubes) joining them are very short. Blood flowing to the lungs from the heart is low in oxygen. It picks up fresh supplies of oxygen in the lungs, then it returns straight to the heart. However the heart is really two muscular pumps stuck together, side by side. Blood going out to the lungs leaves from the right-side pump, but it flows back to the left-side pump.

Thousands of kilometres of blood vessels spread through every body part. At any moment, three-quarters of blood is in the veins, and one-twentieth in the capillaries.

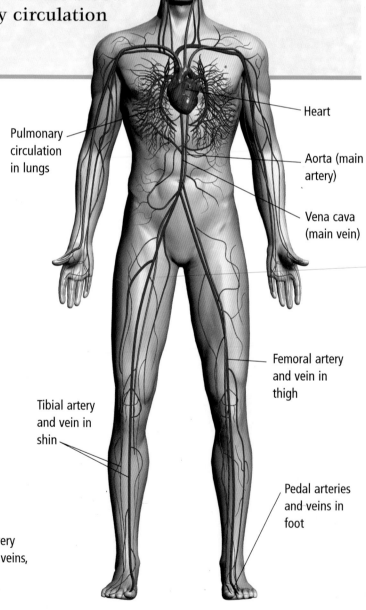

Pulmonary circulation in lungs

Heart

Aorta (main artery)

Vena cava (main vein)

Femoral artery and vein in thigh

Tibial artery and vein in shin

Pedal arteries and veins in foot

Every microscopic cell in the body needs supplies of oxygen and energy, brought by the blood.

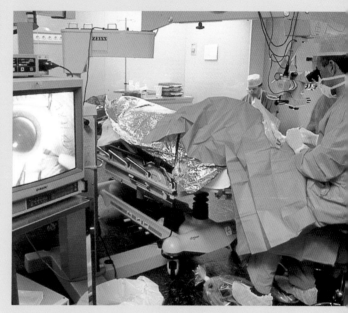
DELIVERING OXYGEN

The left-side pump of the heart sends oxygen-rich blood on a much longer journey, the systemic circulation, to deliver its oxygen all around the body. On its return, the blood is low in oxygen. It flows into the heart's right-side pump. From here it goes off to the lungs, and so the double-circuit is completed, round and round, every minute of life.

BLOOD VESSELS

Arteries

Vessels which carry blood away from the heart are called arteries. They are thick and strong-walled, because the heart pumps out blood at high pressure, which would burst a thin-walled tube. The main artery, taking blood from the left side of the heart, is the aorta. It is thicker than your thumb and blood surges through it at 40 centimetres per second. The arteries divide or branch many times, becoming thinner-walled and narrower as they spread around the body.

Top Tips

Blood from the lower legs and feet must normally flow 'uphill' back to the heart. It is helped by the squeezing actions of the leg muscles during walking and running.

Standing or sitting still for a long time means the leg muscles are not active. So it helps to move the legs, tense their muscles, bend the feet and wiggle the toes, to keep the blood flowing well.

Like the firefighters' hosepipe, the blood system is hydraulic in nature. It depends on liquid being pushed along pipes under pressure – in the body's case, created by the heart.

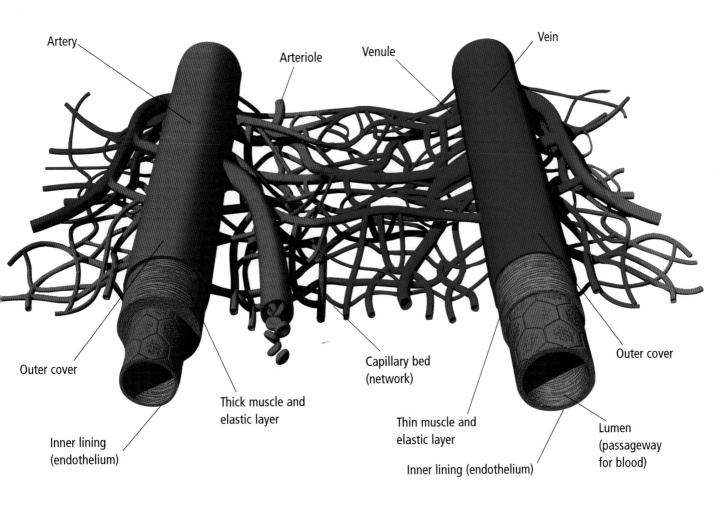

Artery

Arteriole

Venule

Vein

Outer cover

Capillary bed
(network)

Outer cover

Thick muscle and
elastic layer

Thin muscle and
elastic layer

Lumen
(passageway
for blood)

Inner lining
(endothelium)

Inner lining (endothelium)

CAPILLARIES

An artery's smallest branches lead into the next kind of blood vessel, capillaries. These are much thinner than a human hair, and less than one millimetre long, but there are thousands in every body part. The wall of a capillary is only one-thousandth of one millimetre thick. Oxygen, nutrients and other substances can pass through easily, to where they are needed.

VEINS

Capillaries join to form wider tubes, or veins. These have thin, floppy walls, because the blood in them has lost most of its pressure and oozes along slowly.

Arteries have strong, thick, tough walls to withstand blood pressure from the heart. Vein walls are thin and flexible.

The largest veins have one-way, flap-like valves to make sure the blood flows the right way, back to the heart.

MICRO-BODY

The body is made of billions of microscopic parts called cells. A capillary wall is just one cell thick. As oxygen and nutrients seep out from the blood, carbon dioxide and other wastes pass into the blood, to be taken away.

INSIDE BLOOD

A vital liquid

Blood contains at least 200 important substances, and has at least 20 vital jobs. An average adult body is about one-eighth of blood by volume, which is about five litres. Just over half of blood is a liquid called plasma. It is pale yellow and mostly water. But it also contains energy-rich glucose, body salts, minerals, vitamins, nutrients, substances called antibodies that fight germs, and waste materials such as urea and carbon dioxide.

BLOOD CELLS

Every pinhead-sized drop of blood contains five million red cells. Each is shaped like a disc with a pushed-in centre on either side. Its job is to pick up oxygen from the lungs and transport it to other body parts. When red cells collect oxygen they become brighter red. As they give up the oxygen they change to darker reddish-blue. Each drop of blood also contains 10,000 white cells and one-third of a million platelets. Their jobs are shown on page 24.

There are several different kinds of white blood cells (below), also called leucocytes. They vary in size and shape, and in the parts they contain, like the nucleus (cellular control centre). Red cells have no nucleus (below right, on facing page).

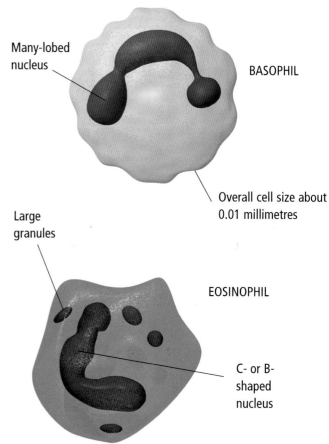

Many-lobed nucleus

BASOPHIL

Overall cell size about 0.01 millimetres

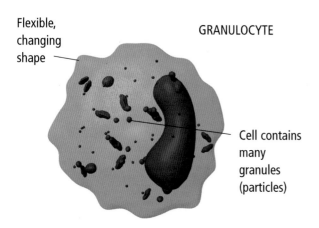

Flexible, changing shape

GRANULOCYTE

Cell contains many granules (particles)

Large granules

EOSINOPHIL

C- or B-shaped nucleus

Top Tips

Different people have slightly different types of blood, called blood groups. They include A, B, AB and 0, and rhesus positive and rhesus negative.

In an emergency, a person's blood can be topped up by blood given, or donated, by someone else. But the donated blood must be the correct group, or it can cause even more problems.

Some people carry a card showing their blood group, so that in an emergency, medical staff can give them the right kind of donated blood more quickly.

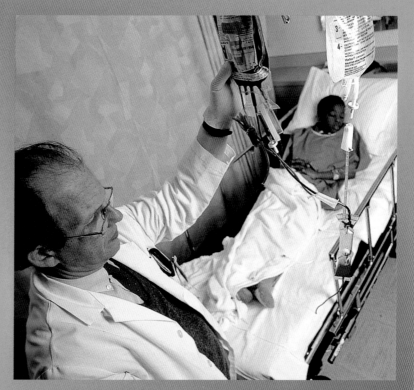

A person may be given whole blood, as a blood tranfusion, or plasma, which is the liquid part of blood with the cells removed. During a major operation, a patient may need 20 litres or more of blood tranfusions.

Overall cell size about 0.007 millimetres

Dished centre

Bulging rim

RED CELLS
(ERYTHROCYTES)

weblinks ↖

To find out more about blood, go to:
www.waylinks.co.uk/series/ourbodies/hlb

ANIMAL VERSUS HUMAN

Blood contains all substances vital for life, which makes it a 'complete food' – because a vampire bat lives on nothing else. It makes a small slit with its razor-sharp front teeth, in a sleeping animal such as a pig or horse, and laps up about 25 millilitres – five teaspoons – of blood.

BLOOD'S JOBS

Vital roles

Blood is a vital delivery service, carrying oxygen, nutrients, minerals and dozens of other substances around the body. It also provides an essential collection service, taking in wastes such as urea for removal by the kidneys, and carbon dioxide to expel in the lungs. Blood also carries body chemicals called hormones. These control processes such as growth, energy use and water balance in the body. Blood helps to keep us in control of our temperature, too. As blood flows, it spreads out heat from busy, warmer parts such as active muscles, to keep the whole body at an even temperature.

FIGHTING DISEASE

White cells are flexible and can change shape. Most help to clean the blood and fight germs. The body makes lots of extra white cells when germs invade during an infection. Some types 'eat' germs whole. Others make natural body chemicals called antibodies, that kill or disable germs. White cells, along with other parts that defend the body against germs and disease, are called the immune system.

SEALING LEAKS

Platelets are involved in clotting. At a cut or wound, platelets swell and become very sticky. They also release

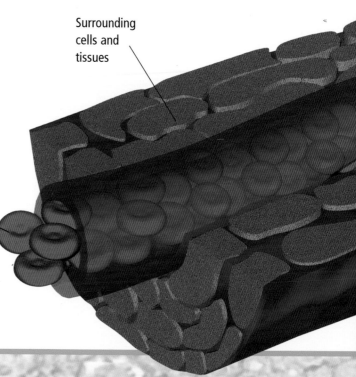

Surrounding cells and tissues

Red blood cells in capillary

A cut or wound in a blood vessel begins a series of chemical changes leading to the formation of a blood clot. Within minutes the leakage is sealed. This type of 'micro-repair' happens every day, all around the body.

chemicals that make thin, sticky, string-like fibres appear in the blood around the wound. The platelets and fibres trap other blood cells and any germs, to form a sticky lump called a clot. This seals the leak. As healing takes place the clot hardens into a scab and falls off.

Top Tips

Blood clots naturally to seal a small cut or wound.

If a small wound is clean, then pressing a pad on it for 10–15 minutes will help the clotting process. Another dressing on top prevents the site being knocked.

Big or dirty cuts need expert attention.

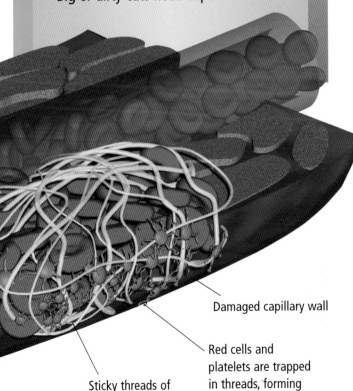

Damaged capillary wall

Red cells and platelets are trapped in threads, forming blood clot

Sticky threads of fibrin appear

MICRO-BODY

Some types of white blood cells, such as macrophages ('big eaters'), can surround a germ such as a bacterium, and take it in or consume it, to destroy it.

Macrophages and similar white blood cells are able to change shape and move about by flowing. This macrophage is flowing around and taking in a foreign particle, which will be digested away.

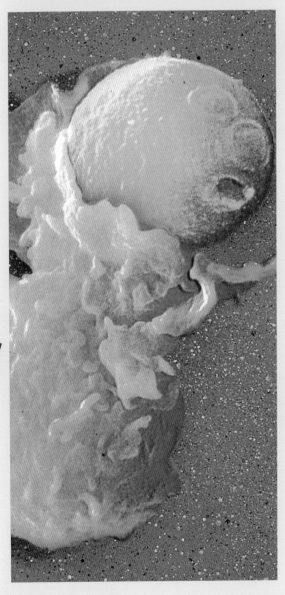

BLOOD AND VESSEL PROBLEMS

Haemophilia

In the blood problem haemophilia, the blood cannot clot properly. This condition runs in families and almost always affects males, although females can be 'carriers' and pass it on to their sons without actually becoming ill themselves. Haemophilia is treated by giving the missing clotting chemicals by injection or in donated blood.

MICRO-BODY

In sickle-cell anaemia, blood's red cells become misshapen and curved or 'sickled'. Sickle cells don't carry oxygen well, and tend to get tangled up, blocking small blood vessels. Sickle-cell anaemia runs in families, and affects people in some ethnic groups more than others.

Sickle-cell anaemia may worsen for a period, which is called a sickle-cell crisis. This may need a stay in hospital. Treatment for this genetic (inherited) condition includes tranfusions of various parts of blood, and medical drugs.

weblinks

To find out more about blood and vessel problems, go to:
www.waylinks.co.uk/series/ourbodies/hlb

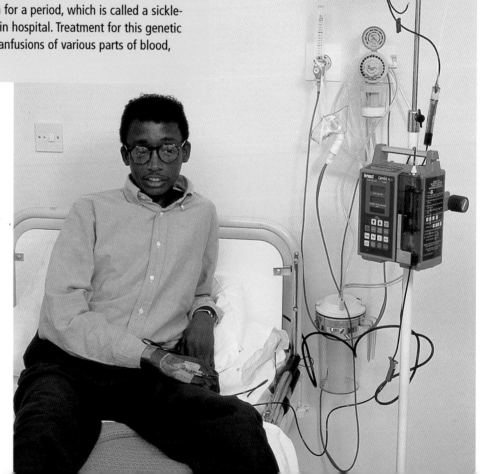

ANAEMIAS

In anaemia, the blood carries less oxygen, so an anaemic person is pale and tired. The oxygen-carrying substance in red cells, haemoglobin, contains the mineral iron. In iron-deficiency anaemia, the body cannot get enough supplies of iron to make new red cells. The problem may be lack of iron in food, something wrong in the way the digestive system takes in iron, or loss of blood from bleeding. Red cells also need the natural chemical vitamin B12. If this is in short supply, perhaps because the body cannot take it in from food, the result is known as pernicious anaemia.

This artery is narrowed and roughened by a lump of fatty material, plaque (atheroma), which has formed within the thickness of its wall. The condition reduces blood flow and makes blood clots within the artery more likely.

LEUKAEMIAS

In most kinds of leukaemias, the blood's white cells multiply out of control. They also lose their disease-fighting abilities, and they 'crowd out' other, normal blood cells, which are made in the jelly-like marrow inside bones. This can lead to pain, serious general illness and increased risk of other diseases. However most kinds of leukaemia can be treated with powerful modern drugs.

BLOOD VESSEL TROUBLE

Atherosclerosis is the formation of sticky patches called plaques in the artery linings. These make less room for blood, slow its flow, and even block the artery. Smoking cigarettes and eating too much food rich in animal fats increases the risk of atherosclerosis. If it affects the arteries to the brain, it can cause the condition known as a stroke.

THE HEART

Appearance

The heart is about as big as the fist of its owner. It is in the middle of the chest, just slightly to the left side, behind the lower breastbone. The 'cage' formed by the breastbone and ribs gives good protection to the heart and, on either side, to the soft, spongy lungs. Like the lungs, the heart is wrapped in a smooth, slippery, oily 'bag'. This is called the pericardium. It lets the heart move smoothly as it squirms and pulses with each heartbeat.

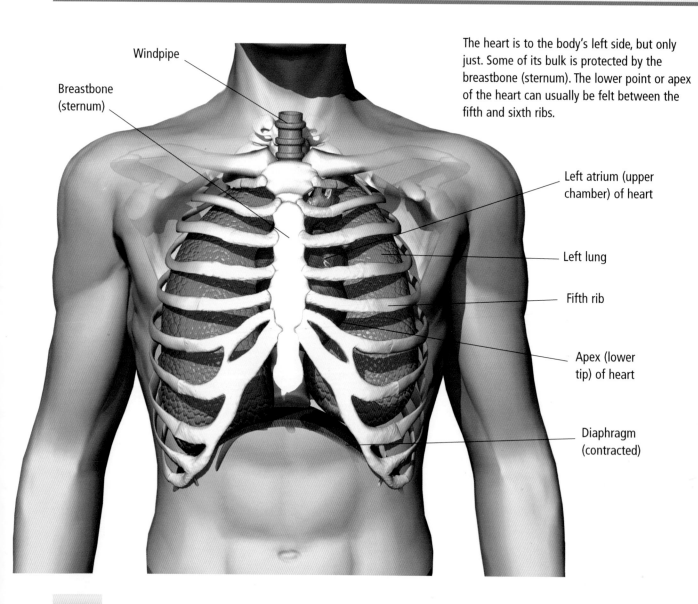

Windpipe

Breastbone
(sternum)

The heart is to the body's left side, but only just. Some of its bulk is protected by the breastbone (sternum). The lower point or apex of the heart can usually be felt between the fifth and sixth ribs.

Left atrium (upper chamber) of heart

Left lung

Fifth rib

Apex (lower tip) of heart

Diaphragm
(contracted)

HEART MUSCLE

The heart is not really heart-shaped. It is more like an upside-down pear, with large blood vessels at the top, and a rounded lower tip called the apex, pointing forwards and to the left. The bulk of the heart is a special type of muscle known as cardiac muscle or myocardium, which forms the thick walls of the heart's inner chambers. Unlike other muscles, such as those in the arms and legs, heart muscle never tires.

CORONARY VESSELS

Any muscle needs plenty of blood to bring it oxygen, energy and nutrients. The heart has its own set of blood vessels, the coronary arteries and veins. The coronary arteries branch across the surface of the heart and angle inwards, into the muscle itself.

The heart's upper parts are mainly connections to the major blood vessels. The lower parts are its muscular-walled pumping chambers. Coronary vessels run over its surface.

ANIMAL VERSUS HUMAN

The biggest animal has the biggest heart. The blue whale's heart is as big as a small family car! But it beats less than 10 times each minute, which is seven or eight times slower than a human heart.

The blue whale's heart pumps blood around its massive, 100-tonne body.

In and out

Each side or pump of the heart has two chambers, separated by a dividing wall, the septum. Blood flows from the main veins into each upper chamber, or atrium. This has thin, flexible walls that balloon out as blood enters. The blood then flows through a flap-like valve into the lower chamber, or ventricle. This is the main pumping chamber with thicker, more muscular walls. The ventricle squeezes hard to force the blood out through another valve, into the main arteries.

VALVES AND WALLS

The left side of the heart, which pumps blood all around the body, has thicker walls than the right ventricle, which only has to send blood to the nearby lungs. The valves in the heart ensure that blood flows the correct way. The chambers and valves are lined with a very smooth layer called endocardium.

This cutaway view shows the four chambers of the heart, and the one-way flaps or valves between them. The upper chambers, atria, have much thinner walls than the lower chambers, ventricles, which provide the main pumping force.

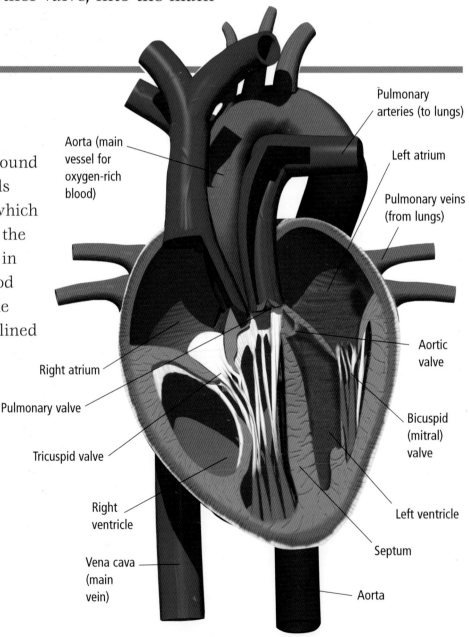

Pulmonary arteries (to lungs)

Left atrium

Pulmonary veins (from lungs)

Aorta (main vessel for oxygen-rich blood)

Aortic valve

Right atrium

Bicuspid (mitral) valve

Pulmonary valve

Tricuspid valve

Left ventricle

Right ventricle

Septum

Vena cava (main vein)

Aorta

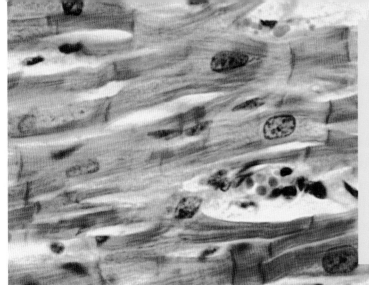

HEARING THE HEART

A doctor listens to the heart's beat through a sound-tube device called a stethoscope. The two main sounds 'lub-dup' are the valves flapping closed. Unusual or extra sounds are sometimes called 'heart murmurs'. They may suggest a problem – or not. Many heart murmurs are 'innocent' and not the sign of a problem.

NEW HEARTS

For some heart problems, the only treatment may be a 'new' heart. This is usually a healthy heart from a person who has died of other causes. It is connected into the patient's body during a long operation. In some cases the original heart is left in place and the new heart is added, 'piggyback' style. Mechanical hearts, built of metal and plastic, have also been tried.

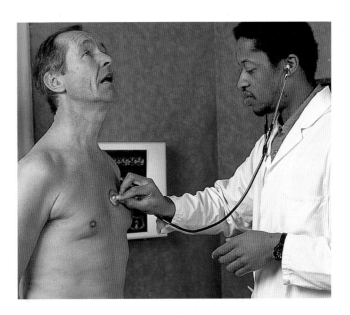

The heart's beating sounds pass through the chest wall to the skin, where they can be heard through a stethoscope.

Try this!

Pretend your fist is your heart. Hold it just under some water and make it 'beat' once each second by opening and closing your fingers. Can you squirt out water, like heart pumps blood? How long could you keep this fist-heart beating?

weblinks

To find out more about the heart, go to:
www.waylinks.co.uk/series/ourbodies/hlb

HOW THE HEART BEATS

Squeezing and relaxing

Each heartbeat is a double-action of squeezing hard to force blood out, then relaxing to fill again. The squeezing is called systole ('siss-toe-lee'). It begins at the lower tip of the heart and passes upwards, to push the blood up from the lower ventricles, through the valves and into the main arteries. The powerful muscle contraction makes the blood surge into the arteries with great force. The pressure travels as a bulge or pulsation in the artery wall, out through all the arteries around the body.

RELAX AND REFILL

After its powerful contraction, the heart relaxes. The valves close to prevent blood flowing back in from the arteries. Instead, blood oozes in slowly from the veins, to fill the heart chambers. During this stage, diastole ('die-ass-toe-lee'), blood pressure in the heart and the whole circulatory system is at its lowest.

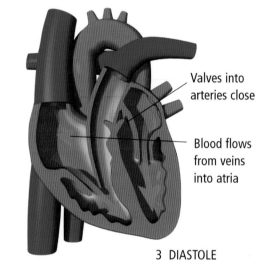

Valves into arteries close

Blood flows from veins into atria

3 DIASTOLE

The phase of the heartbeat when the heart relaxes and fills with blood is called diastole. The pumping phase is known as systole.

1 ATRIAL SYSTOLE

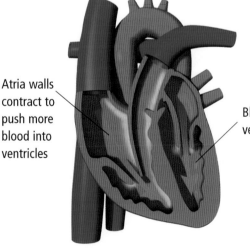

Atria walls contract to push more blood into ventricles

Blood fills ventricles

2 VENTRICULAR SYSTOLE

Blood flows from ventricles into arteries

Valves between atria and ventricles close

Ventricle walls contract

THE PACEMAKER

The heart has a natural pacemaker – a control centre for the heartbeat. This is the sino-atrial node, in the upper part of the right atrium. It sends out tiny natural electrical signals along special muscle fibres. These work like 'wires' to carry the signals into the heart muscle, for the squeezing part of the heartbeat. The natural pacemaker has its own rhythm of sending out signals. But this is usually altered by nerve messages from the brain (see page 36).

ANIMAL VERSUS HUMAN

In general, smaller animals have hearts that beat faster. The shrew's heart beats more than 300 times each minute – five times per second!

The shrew's heart and whole body work so fast, this creature may die if without food for six hours.

MICRO-BODY

The heart's 'wiring' is made of special muscle fibres called Purkinje fibres. These carry tiny electrical signals from the natural pacemaker to the heart muscle, to make it beat.

Purkinje fibres are large types of muscle fibres. However they are specialized, not to contract (shorten), but to carry electrical signals.

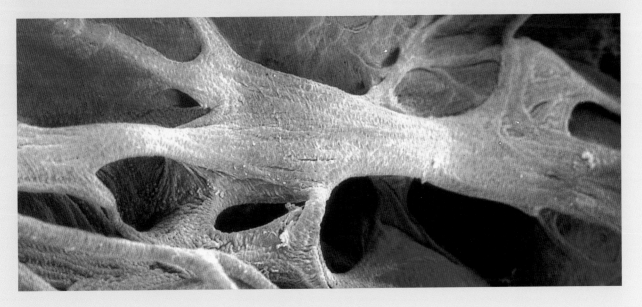

WHEN THE HEART POUNDS

CHANGING PACE

The heart does not beat steadily at the same rate, all the time. Its beating rate, and the amount of blood it pumps, alter for different conditions. For example, if the body is active, running or playing sports, the muscles need more oxygen and energy. So the heart beats faster and harder to send more blood to them.

HOW MUCH BLOOD?

At rest, an average heart beats about 70 times per minute, and pumps 70 millilitres of blood each time. So it pumps around five litres of blood in one minute – which is all the blood in the body. We can count the heart rate by counting the wrist pulse (see panel on page 35).

Blood pressure is measured accurately by a medical device called a sphygmomanometer, or a modern electronic version.

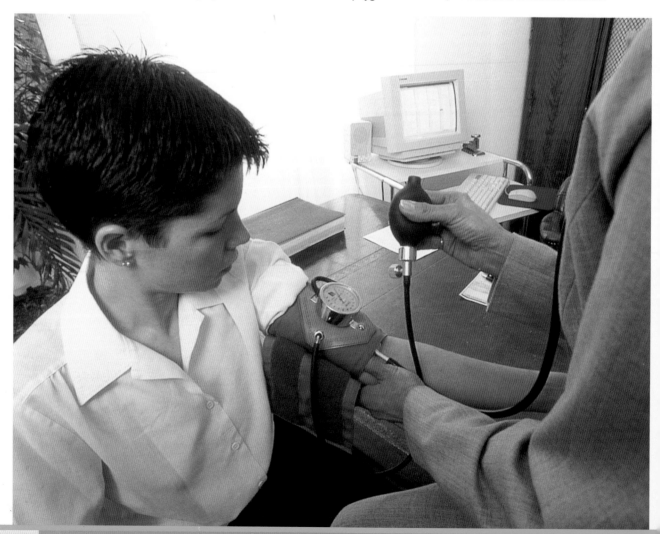

FASTER AND HARDER

During exercise or activity, the brain sends nerve messages to the heart, telling its natural pacemaker to speed the beat greatly (see page 36). The rate can increase to more than 150 beats per minute. Also each beat during such activity is more powerful, sending out twice the normal amount of blood. These two effects mean the heart pumps far more blood than it does at rest – 20 litres per minute or more. We can feel the faster, harder beats inside the chest, and we say the heart 'thumps' or 'pounds'.

RECOVERY

After exercise, the body rests and recovers. The heart rate and the amount of blood pumped both decrease. The time taken for the heartbeat to return to the resting rate is called the recovery time. In general, the fitter and healthier the body, the shorter the recovery time.

weblinks

To find out more about the heart rate, go to:
www.waylinks.co.uk/series/ourbodies/hlb

The pulsing of the arteries can be felt at various places on the body, in addition to the usual site in the wrist, which is the radial artery.

Temporal pulse

Facial pulse

Carotid pulse

Radial pulse

Brachial pulse

Try this!

Feel for your pulse with the tip of your forefinger. Press gently on the inside of the wrist, in the soft area just below the base of the thumb. Each pulse is the wave of pressure from a heartbeat passing along the arteries. The pulse rate is the number of pulses in one minute, and is the same as the heart rate.

CONTROLLING THE HEART AND LUNGS

Messages

Each heartbeat is set off by the heart's own pacemaker. But this is under the control of messages from the brain. The brain also sends out messages to control the breathing muscles. Both of these processes speed up during exercise or sport, to supply the body muscles with more blood containing oxygen and energy.

THE BRAIN IN CONTROL

Sensors in and near the brain detect the pressure of the blood, the amount of oxygen it contains, and even more important, the amount of the waste gas carbon dioxide. As the level of carbon dioxide rises, and the level of oxygen falls, the brain sends signals from its breathing centre to the breathing muscles, to make them work harder and faster. In a similar way, the brain's heartbeat centre sends messages to the heart, to make it beat faster and more powerfully.

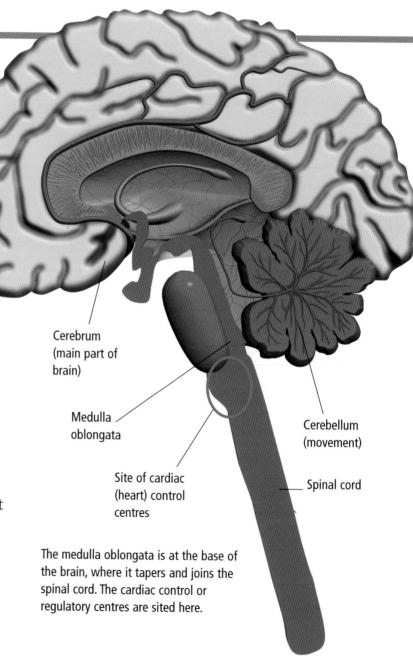

Cerebrum (main part of brain)

Medulla oblongata

Site of cardiac (heart) control centres

Cerebellum (movement)

Spinal cord

The medulla oblongata is at the base of the brain, where it tapers and joins the spinal cord. The cardiac control or regulatory centres are sited here.

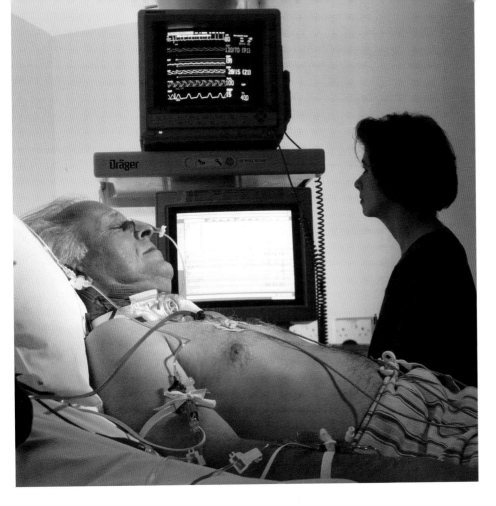

In a hospital intensive care unit, the vital signs monitor screen shows a constantly updated display of a patient's heartbeat rate, blood pressure, breathing rate and other essential body functions.

CHEMICAL CONTROL

The heart is controlled by nerves – and by chemicals. These are natural body chemicals called hormones, made by parts called glands. The adrenal glands, one above each kidney, make the hormone adrenaline. This is released into the blood when you are in a frightening, stressful or exciting situation. Adrenaline affects many parts of the body, to get it ready for action. In particular, it makes the heart beat harder and faster, to pump more blood. This is why a sudden fright or worry makes the heart 'thump' or 'pound' in the chest.

ANIMAL VERSUS HUMAN

When a seal dives, it has to hold its breath, and can no longer take in oxygen. But the seal has special muscles which store extra supplies of oxygen. This means that the seal can stay underwater for a long time – perhaps more than 10 minutes.

As a seal dives its heart rate slows, to use less oxygen, so that its swimming muscles can use more oxygen.

A CHECK-UP FOR THE HEART AND LUNGS

SOUNDS

Regular medical tests almost always include a check on the heart and lungs, because they are so important to general health. The doctor listens to the heartbeat and breathing with a stethoscope (see page 31). Wheezy breathing could suggest a lung infection or asthma. A heartbeat may be too fast or slow, or not regular. This can be treated by an artificial pacemaker – a small electronic device put into the body and connected by wires to the heart, to control its beating.

A pacemaker can be fitted into the chest wall, under the loose skin and flesh of the breast and armpit area.

Top Tips

Heart and lung diseases mainly affect adults. But harm can start in childhood, from too little exercise and too many fatty foods. Developing good habits early, such as exercising regularly, choosing healthy foods, and not smoking or taking other drugs, can help to avoid damage later.

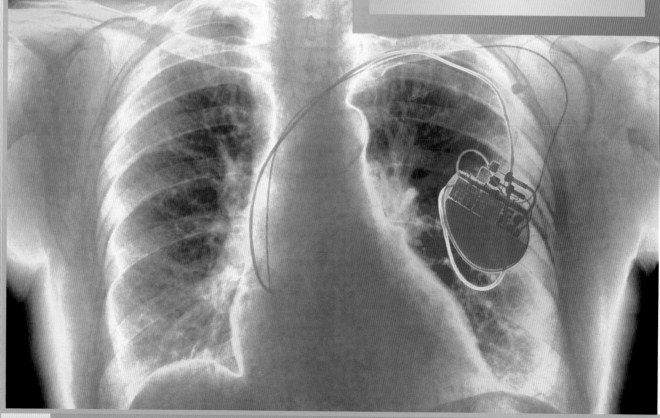

THE ELECTRIC HEART

Beating heart muscles send out tiny 'waves' of electricity through the body. Sensor pads on the skin detect these waves, which are shown on a screen or traced onto a paper strip, by an ECG (electrocardiograph) machine. The spikes and dips in the wave patterns reveal many kinds of heart trouble.

The ability of the lungs to blow out hard depends on the strength of the breathing muscles, and also on the vital capacity – the total amount of air the lungs can hold when fully inflated and then expel with force.

BLOOD PRESSURE

Blood pressure tests can detect many health problems. A collar-like cuff containing an inflatable bag is placed around the upper arm or another body part and is blown up with air. The doctor (or a machine) detects when the cuff's pressure is high enough to stop blood flowing through the nearest artery, known as systolic pressure (see page 32). Then the cuff's pressure is reduced so that blood can flow continuously, which is diastolic pressure.

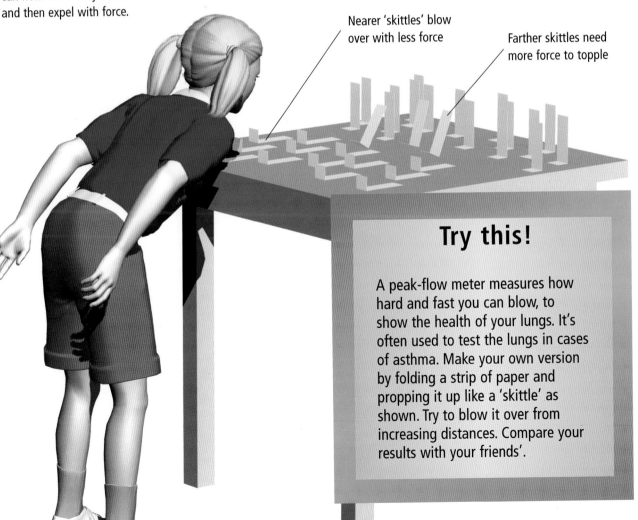

Nearer 'skittles' blow over with less force

Farther skittles need more force to topple

Try this!

A peak-flow meter measures how hard and fast you can blow, to show the health of your lungs. It's often used to test the lungs in cases of asthma. Make your own version by folding a strip of paper and propping it up like a 'skittle' as shown. Try to blow it over from increasing distances. Compare your results with your friends'.

A baby's lifeline

Inside the mother's womb, a baby cannot breathe or eat. It receives oxygen and nutrients from its mother along a 'lifeline', the umbilical cord. Blood vessels in the cord connect the baby's circulatory system to a part called the afterbirth or placenta, in the wall of the womb. The baby's blood flows along the cord to the placenta, takes in oxygen and nutrients, then flows back. As the baby emerges into the outside world at birth, it suddenly starts to breathe, as its lungs fill with air. Also the placenta comes away from the wall of the womb and can no longer supply oxygen or nutrients. So the baby's lungs, heart and circulation must change rapidly.

Before birth, 'bypass' blood vessels mean that little blood flows to the lungs or digestive system, since these do not work in the womb. The umbilical vessels bring oxygen and nutrients.

BEFORE BIRTH

While the baby was growing in the womb, blood flowed through an opening between the right and left atria (upper chambers) of its heart. This meant very little blood went from the heart to the lungs. It did not matter because the lungs were not working. Also a small 'bypass' artery took any blood heading for the lungs and carried it directly to the main artery for the body.

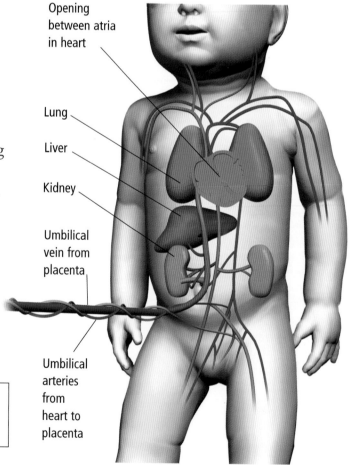

Opening between atria in heart

Lung

Liver

Kidney

Umbilical vein from placenta

Umbilical arteries from heart to placenta

─── **weblinks** ───

To find out more about the heart before and after birth, go to: www.waylinks.co.uk/series/ourbodies/hlb

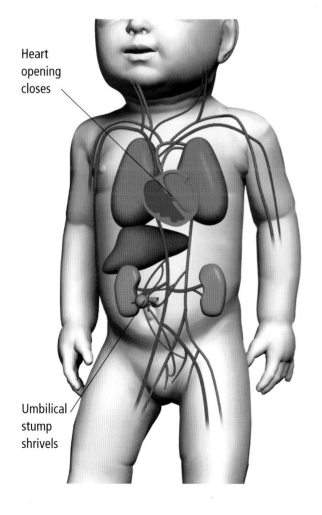

A new baby has a thorough medical check-up, which includes listening to the heart and lungs through the device called a stethoscope.

Heart opening closes

Umbilical stump shrivels

ANIMAL VERSUS HUMAN

When a baby whale is born, it needs to breathe air, like a human baby. Its mother may nudge it to the surface, so it can start to breathe more easily.

A newborn whale has the instinct to swim up for breaths of air. But it splutters at first, while helped by its mother.

AFTER BIRTH

At birth, both the atrial opening and bypass close quickly. Blood flows to the heart's right side, and so to the lungs for oxygen. In rare cases this does not happen and the baby has trouble breathing. This is one form of 'hole in the heart'. The baby's blood and body cells lack oxygen and this gives its skin a blue tinge ('blue baby'). The problem can usually be cured by an operation to close the hole. Another change at birth is that the vessels to the umbilical cord shrink rapidly, and the cord is cut or soon drops off the baby's abdomen.

After birth, the opening or 'window' between the two sides of the heart closes. So does the bypass artery between the pulmonary and systemic circulations.

HEART PROBLEMS

Narrowing and hardening

The coronary arteries, which supply the heart muscle with blood, are small but vital. Several problems can affect them. These include narrowing by fatty plaque (atherosclerosis), as described on page 27. The artery walls may also harden and stiffen (arteriosclerosis), so they no longer bulge to cope with the blood's surges of pressure.

BLOOD CLOTS AND HEART ATTACK

Coronary artery disease is one of the biggest health problems in the modern world. In some regions, it leads to one in every three deaths. Narrowed, stiffened arteries reduce the blood supply that takes oxygen and nutrients to the heart muscle. They also increase the risk of coronary thrombosis, when blood clots in a coronary artery and blocks it. If blood cannot get through, the heart muscle stops working. This is one form of heart attack.

One way to restart a stopped heart is to pass electrical signals through it, using a medical machine known as a defibrillator. The signals travel between two large plates, or electrodes, placed on the chest.

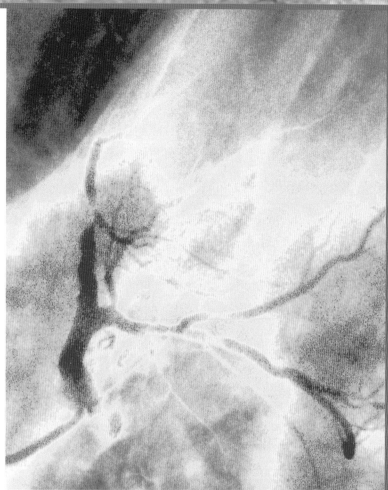

This image, called a coronary angiogram, shows the heart's coronary vessels, branching into the heart muscle. The basic image can be colour-coded by computer to reveal details more clearly.

SEEING THE HEART'S VESSELS

The coronary vessels can be seen by a test called a coronary angiogram or arteriogram. A special chemical which shows up on an X-ray screen is put into the blood near the heart, through a long tube known as a catheter. The doctors watch the screen to see any narrowed parts or blockages as blood flows through the coronary arteries. Some other types of scan, such as CT (computerized tomography) and MR (magnetic resonance) also show details of the heart and lungs.

Try this!

Look at an old kettle or piece of water pipe. See how hard minerals called 'scale' or 'fur' can collect inside. Unhealthy blood vessels can suffer in a similar way, blocked by the fatty substance, plaque.

CURING HEART PROBLEMS

Many medical drugs and operations treat heart problems. In balloon angioplasty, a thin tube with a balloon-like tip is put into the narrowed artery. The tip is inflated to stretch and widen the vessel. In a coronary bypass operation, less important blood vessels from other body parts, such as in the legs, are used to bypass narrowed or blocked coronary arteries.

weblinks

To find out more about heart problems, go to:
www.waylinks.co.uk/series/ourbodies/hlb

A HEALTHY HEART AND LUNGS

The importance of exercise

Exercise and sport keep muscles active, strong and healthy, rather than weak and wasting away. This is true of the muscles in the arms and legs – and the heart and breathing muscles too. Activity should make the heart beat faster and more powerfully, and cause some breathlessness, so the lungs, breathing and circulatory system work harder. However, each person should take medical advice before exercise, and then train gradually, to become fitter. It can be dangerous to put the lungs and heart under too much strain, too suddenly.

During an exercise ECG, a person undergoes activity such as jogging on a treadmill, while sensors record the heart's electrical signals.

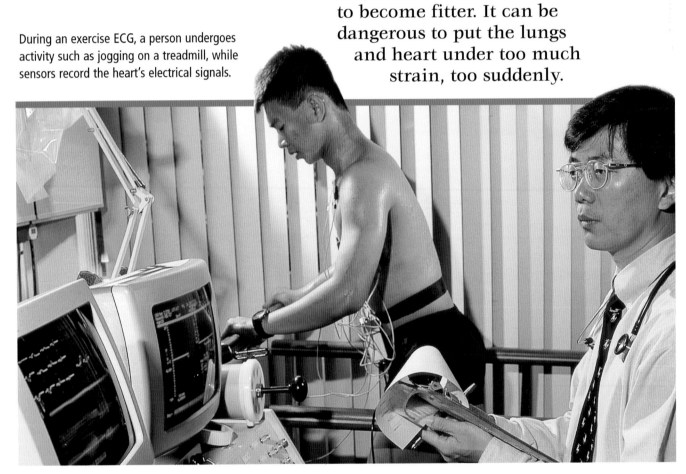

EATING AND HEALTH

Many surveys show a connection between eating too many fat-rich foods, especially animal fats, and problems of the heart and blood vessels. In particular, too much of the fatty substance called cholesterol in the blood can cause heart and blood vessel problems in certain people. Healthy eating includes plenty of fresh fruit and vegetables, which benefit all parts of the body.

Try this!

Write down a list of what you eat for a few days. Are your meals healthy and helping your body? Too many fatty foods and processed foods, especially fatty meats, are less healthy. Plenty of fresh vegetables and fruits are more healthy.

SMOKING AND ILLNESS

Fumes, dust and particles in air can be breathed into the lungs and cause damage. This is why workers in some jobs, such as in chemical factories or mines, often wear facemasks and air filters. Yet other people cause immense damage to their own lungs, heart, blood vessels and many other body parts, and do it on purpose, by smoking tobacco.

Top Tips

There's an exercise, sport or activity for almost everyone, which will help the heart and lungs stay fit and healthy. How about swimming, workouts at home or in the gym, basketball, cycling, dance, football, tennis, and of course, extreme high-altitude express formation skyboarding ...

Snowboarding makes the heart beat faster because the body is using many muscles – and because it's a very exciting activity!

GLOSSARY

alveolus One of the microscopic air spaces or 'air bubbles' inside the lungs. Oxygen from air is absorbed into the blood flowing around an alveolus.

anaemia When the blood cannot carry sufficient oxygen for the body's needs. There are various forms of anaemia with different causes and treatments.

arteriole A small blood vessel formed by the repeated branching or dividing of an artery.

artery A blood vessel with thick, muscular walls that carries blood under high pressure away from the heart.

atheroma A fatty substance that forms as lumps in the walls of blood vessels, causing them to become narrowed or even blocked (atherosclerosis).

bronchiole A small airway in the lungs, formed by the repeated branching or dividing of a bronchus.

bronchus A main airway in the lungs, formed by the branching or dividing of the windpipe (trachea).

capillary The smallest type of blood vessel, much thinner than a human hair, with walls only one cell thick.

carbon dioxide A gas formed from the breakdown of nutrients inside the body to obtain energy for life processes. Carbon dioxide is poisonous if allowed to accumulate within the body.

cardiac To do with the heart.

cell A single unit or 'building block' of life - the human body is made of billions of cells of many different kinds.

circulatory system The parts of the body including the heart, blood vessels and blood, that are specialized to deliver oxygen, glucose and other vital substances around the body, and to collect waste substances.

coronary To do with the coronary blood vessels, which supply the heart muscle with blood.

diaphragm A dome-shaped muscle under the lungs, forming the base of the chest; it is the main breathing muscle.

diastole Part of the heartbeat cycle when the heart relaxes and refills with blood from the veins.

erythrocyte A red blood cell that is specialized to carry oxygen.

haemoglobin The substance in red blood cells that carries oxygen. Haemoglobin contains iron and when it is joined to oxygen it is bright red in colour.

hormones The natural body chemicals made by parts called endocrine glands. Hormones circulate in blood and control many processes such as growth, the use of energy, water balance and the formation of urine.

leucocyte The general name for a white blood cell - there are many different kinds with specialized tasks such as eating germs.

oxygen A gas making up one-fifth of air, which has no colour, taste or smell, but which is vital for breaking down nutrients inside the body to obtain energy for life processes.

pericardium The outer bag-like covering of the heart, which is slippery and lubricates the heart's beating motions.

plasma The liquid part of blood, with the cells taken away.

pleurae The outer bag-like coverings of the lungs, which are slippery and lubricate the lungs' breathing motions.

pulmonary circulation The flow of blood from the heart to the lungs and back ('pulmonary' means to do with the lungs).

pulse rate The number of high-pressure pulsations per minute, usually felt in the artery of the wrist, caused by the heart's beating - the pulse rate is the same as the heartbeat rate.

respiratory system The parts of the body including the nose, throat, windpipe, bronchial airways and lungs, that are specialized to take in air and absorb oxygen from it.

systemic circulation The flow of blood from the heart, around the body (but not to the lungs) and back.

systole The part of the heartbeat cycle when the heart muscle contracts powerfully to pump blood at high pressure into the arteries.

terminal bronchiole The smallest type of airway in the lungs, formed by the repeated branching or dividing of a bronchiole, and leading to a group of air spaces or alveoli.

trachea The windpipe, which conveys air from the throat, down through the neck into the chest.

valve The pocket- or flap-like parts in a tube that allow fluid to flow only one way. The valves in the main veins and heart control the direction of flow of the blood.

vein A blood vessel with thin walls that carries blood under low pressure back to the heart.

venule A small blood vessel formed by joining or merging of capillaries.

FURTHER INFORMATION

BOOKS

The Circulatory System, Pam Walker, Elaine Wood (Lucent Books, 2002)

The Respiratory System, Helen Frost (Pebble Books, 2001)

Respiration and Circulation, Andreu Llamas, Luis Rizo (Gareth Stevens, 1998)

Your Blood, Anita Ganeri (Gareth Stevens, 2002)

Blood, Steve Parker, Ian Thompson (Illustrator), Mark Iley (Illustrator) (Copper Beech Books, 1997)

ORGANIZATIONS

British Heart Foundation
The leading UK charity fighting heart and circulatory problems

Head Office
14 Fitzhardinge Street
London W1H 6DH
Tel: 020 7935 0185
Email: internet@bhf.org.uk

National Asthma Campaign
Head Office
Providence House
Providence Place
London N1 0NT
Tel: 020 7226 2260

Scottish Office
2a North Charlotte Street
Edinburgh EH2 4HR
Tel: 0131 226 2544

Asthma Helpline 0845 7 01 02 03

National Blood Service (UK)
Tel: 0845 7 711 711
See leaflets at health centres, hospitals and other medical premises for local offices and details on where and when to give blood, bone marrow and tissue donation, and information on what happens to donated blood.

INDEX